THE FORMULA FOR MAKING A

IN TWELVE MONTHS

IT'S ALL IN THE NUMBERS

MICHAEL TEAGUE

THE AUTHOR

Hi, I'm Michael. I'm an Internet Entrepreneur, Transformational Speaker, and Spiritual Leader. My goal is to provide you with help, hope, and healing, with the content I provide. My personal mission is to do well, by doing good, to all of humanity

DISCLAIMER

This work is sold with the understanding that neither the author nor the publisher are held responsible for the results accrued from the advice in this book

FOREWORD

I am writing this E-Book for anyone who wants to be a Millionaire in the next twelve months, especially those, who are Internet Entrepreneurs. For those of us who have embraced the frustrating, enervating, sometimes disappointing, yet exhilarating world of Entrepreneurship, this book is for you.

I salute you!

CONTENTS

- The Beginning

- Let's get Started

- The Formula

- In Addition to The Numbers

- What Next

- Some Practical Ways

- The Final Words

THE BEGINNING

My name is Michael. I have wanted to be rich all of my life, and so I started a million dollar plan at twenty-one. Here I stand, at fifty-six, poised to make over $1 million within the next twelve months. I have The Formula, and I want to share that formula with you, but let us learn more about that later. Between then and now, what have I had going on? I attended college and graduate school. Then, I spent the first part of my working career in the faith-based industry (a lot of meaning, but no money). The second part of my career, however, has been in corporate healthcare. Eighteen years ago, I started in an entry-level position. Over the next five years, I rose to the level of Director (a big title, not much more money). Then, that company declared bankruptcy, and I was able to start work at another, but this time in sales. I have had four years of hell in sales, yet I also have earned a hell of a lot of money! Now, as a six-figure earner (titles are important), I am developing a National Healthcare Start-Up.

Here is another part of my journey: I am an entrepreneur. More importantly, I am an entrepreneur with over eleven ventures, including inventions, in cue. Mark Cuban, owner of the Dallas Mavericks; Shark Tank Guru; and Billionaire, said this: "It only takes one time to get it right, to enjoy phenomenal success." I have figured it out. It took fourteen years of successes, failures, and mistakes. It also took a book, a speaking business; a billion-dollar invention that I had to walk away from (I am still going to make it, I just had to leave my partner); several network marketing opportunities; and a dissolved and re-started entertainment company, yet I have figured it out. I have invested tens of thousands of dollars in myself. I have been mentored by Larry Ellison, Bill Gates, 50 Cent, Sean "P Diddy" Combs, Jay-Z, Tai Lopez, Grant Cardone, Warren Buffet, Steven Jobs, and the like. Pause. How so? I have bought their books and read articles about them! Now, I am ready to make my first million. Most importantly, I have figured it out. I have cracked the million dollar code. Even more important than this, I want to take you on my journey. Why? Your success is more important than mine. Why? As Russell Simmons said: "Good givers are great getters." Why? As they say on the streets: "Ain't no fun, if the homies can't have none!" Why? As one of the greatest spiritual teachers in human history said: "To whom much is given, much shall be required." And so, I want to share with you my formula, and then some effective strategies that will result in over $1 million in revenue over the next twelve months. Let us get started!

<u>LET'S GET STARTED</u>

Thank you, first and foremost, for purchasing this e-book. I wrote it to provide you with the formula to achieve a $1 million level of revenue. In my own pursuit of $ 1 million dollars in revenue goals, let me list what I have tried and why they do not guarantee this success. I have purchased "systems." I am sure that you have seen numerous "systems" advertised on Instagram, Facebook, YouTube, or all of the above. "Systems" abound in any and every industry imaginable, however, "systems" do not always work. The majority of the revenue is generated by the one who created the "system". He/she makes money by selling you their "system," rather than experiencing successes based upon the product or service, which they are selling the "system" for! Perhaps you fall into the category of those who have purchased "systems", only to be frustrated when they failed to help you to achieve your dream of $1 million in revenue.

I have had many ideas. I have written them down, put them on my dream board, and discussed them with people that I trust. However, contrary to widespread belief, ideas do not make money. Ideas, when backed by solid business plans, as well as sufficient financing and a formidable team, can make money. Perhaps, you are like me. I have had business partners, who acted more like employees than partners. As a result, I had to sever those partnerships, and "go it alone." This adage still remains true: "It takes money to make money." Honestly, even though I've boot-strapped several business ventures, I have lacked sufficient financing for those ventures to gain traction. Without sufficient financing to execute them, even strong business plans will rarely yield results. Can you relate to what I am saying?

Lastly, but not least, I've purchased products primarily in the Network Marketing Industry. I like network marketing because this business model requires little capital investment, offers sales training and mentoring, as well as a tried-and-true business model. I have purchased nutritional products, consumer products, travel services, and the like with little to no success. High-pressure sales tactics, notwithstanding network marketing, can yield some success. For those of you who have either considered or participated in network marketing businesses, it takes two to five years and requires ten, twenty hours per week to generate a full-time income. By the way, that is a formula. This is why I like formulas. Products will not sell if there is no market for them regardless of the entrepreneur's passion for them. This is called "Proof of Concept." Products which offer no viable value to the marketplace will not sell.

So, for me, and perhaps even for you, "systems", ideas, and products have not yielded results. This is what I have discovered: All business success is driven by the numbers. Another word for numbers is metrics or formula. So like the network marketing numbers that I mentioned earlier, all business boils down to numbers. Be aware that these are numbers that will drive a $1 million revenue, and these numbers will result in a guaranteed formula to achieve that goal.

THE FORMULA

If you do not believe that this formula works, take out a calculator and test the formula. Remember, I promised you a money-back guarantee if the numbers do not work. Yes, the numbers work so please, keep reading.

So, you have the formula: 5,000 customers, who pay $20.00/month, over a twelve-month period to yield $1.2 million. That is $240.00/year per customer. That is affordable. Now that you know that the numbers work, you can calculate revenue over multiple years. I am already excited for you!

Now that you have The Formula, let us talk about the Industry. The industry that I am speaking of is the Digital Economy. In human history, we have gone through three ages, and have now arrived at a fourth. We started with the Agricultural Age. Then, we progressed to the Industrial Age. We passed from the Industrial Age, to the Information Age. After the Information Age, we now have arrived at the Digital Industry Age.

Let me give you an example of how the Digital Economy works. I live in New Jersey, yet the supplier for my e-commerce business is from China. The supplier's company, *Hypersku*, can source from all over the world. Through the online platform *Upwork*, I have secured a Graphic/Web Designer from India and can hire other freelance workers from anywhere in the world. By means of social media platforms such as Facebook, Instagram, and YouTube, you and I can create ads reaching targeted audiences globally. So, I have chosen the Digital Economy to make my money. An article by *statistica.com* presents the following information regarding the Digital Economy:

- Digital Revenue is projected to reach $571.22 billion in 2021
- The United Arab Emirates; South Korea; Norway; Luxembourg; Iceland; and the US have a total Internet Penetration (the percentage of the population that utilizes the Internet) of 92.1%
- The top five (5) online stores by e-commerce net sales (first-party sales) of Amazon.com; Walmart.com; Apple.com; HomeDepot.com; and BestBuy.com have a combined $121.3 billion in net sales.

As we can see, the Digital Economy is a powerful economic engine which impacts the global world. More importantly, we can have a piece of that revenue.

You can leverage the resources of the Digital Economy to implement The Formula. I need to share with you the methodology. First, the methodology requires a direct-to-consumer approach. It also involves an understanding of direct marketing. Finally, it needs us to understand the purchase cycle, as well as the total number of people who will be advertised to. The bottom line is: It is all in the numbers.

Here is The Formula: 5,000 x $20.00 x 12 = $1.2 Million

This shows 5,000 customers, who spend $20.00 per month, over a twelve-month period. Here is another way of looking at this: 5,000 customers who spend $240.00 in a year. So, everybody you have the numbers; they all work out. I just showed you the formula for making 1.2 million dollars; think about that. You do not have to buy a "system". You do not have to buy a course. You don't have to go to a workshop or listen to a guru. All you need is the numbers.

IN ADDITION TO THE NUMBERS

I wanted to start with the numbers because numbers do not lie. In addition to the numbers, there are some other things that you need. Part of this $1.2 million digital marketing approach requires that you communicate directly with the consumer via online marketing. So we are talking about Facebook, Instagram, Snapchat, or TikToK ads. We are also talking about SEO, as well as pay-per-click. In this digital age, specifically in this digital economy, the key to instant and ongoing revenue is to communicate directly with the consumer. Why? This is because you are bypassing the middleman and bypassing the retail establishments. You are bypassing everything in favor of communicating directly with the consumer. This implies a couple of things: 1) You are communicating with them; 2) A certain percentage will buy, which will comprise the baseline for your calculation; and 3) You continue to communicate with them as well as provide good customer service so that they will continue buying. This is how you grow revenue.

Daymond John, the founder of FUBU, and one of the original participants on Shark Tank, stated that there are only three ways that your grow revenue: 1) Grow your customer base; 2) Upsell your current customer base; or 3) You create an incentive for your current customer base to buy more frequently. You can do this via the Digital Economy. The chief way to do this is to continue to provide value. You need to provide products that cost increasingly more. In this way you're not only meeting their needs first, but you're also going to increase the baseline, or percentage, of those people who buy the product or service. This results in an increase in the amount of revenue that comes to you, because an increasing baseline of the people are buying. Does that make sense?

Let us look at some examples. Amazon, for instance, started by Jeff Bezos. Doesn't Jeff Bezos use a direct-to-consumer approach? I've bought from Amazon; I am sure that you bought from Amazon. As a matter of fact, Jeff Bezos and the shareholders of Amazon are about to get incredibly happy because, as I write this book, we're approaching the holiday season! Through online advertising, as well as various other means of advertising, Jeff Bezos is driving people to the Amazon website where you can purchase literally any and everything!

Let us look at another example: Apple. Whether it is their consumer products, and/or their music, it is a direct-to-consumer approach. You do not have to go through a middleman to get to your songs or to create your playlist or to buy anything from Apple through Amazon. Are you beginning to see the genius of the direct-to-consumer approach? So now, I have to give credit where it is due. The first person that I heard of talk about the power of a direct-to-consumer approach was Damon Dash. You may not know who Damon Dash is; if so, allow me to let you know. Damon Dash is an entrepreneur/former hip-hop mogul. Ironically enough, he is the man who discovered Jay-Z and Kanye West. He is also one of the co-founders of *RocaWear*, a clothing brand. Now, he is a diversified entrepreneur who, from my understanding, has stepped away from the music industry. He discussed several years ago the power of a direct-to-consumer approach.

Another example includes the followers and friends options on social media sites as the new human capital. Listen to what I've said: followers and friends on social media sites are the new human capital. For example, in 2014, Sony paid Kevin Hart two million dollars in order to promote the movie *No Good Deed* to his Twitter followers! At the time, Kevin had 14.8 million Twitter followers. You and I also have an opportunity to build a significant social media following. We can use Facebook, Instagram, Snapchat, TikTok, as well as any other form of social media to develop that following. We can use online advertising to reach the world, literally!

Let me say, as an aside, although I am focusing on the online marketplace, The Formula also works with offline marketing. So if you have five thousand customers, each of whom spend $20 per month, over a 12-month period that is 1.2 million dollars, also! The difficulty, as well as the challenge, is to find a place ("Brick and Mortar"); lease that space; use advertising in order to attract customers to your location; build a five thousand person consumer base; and then, get them to spend $20 a month over 12-month period. I am only citing this so that you know that The Formula works in both the online and offline spaces. That said, for those of you who are enamored with brick and mortar, let us look at this. We know that the pandemic has significantly reduced our ability to congregate. We also know that the pandemic has caused a disruption in the economy, and that people are being laid off left and right. This results in less foot traffic to the retail establishments, and thus, less revenue whether the advertising is either online or offline. Here is the thing: retail establishments are quickly becoming a thing of the past. For example, Tai Lopez, a social media marketing guru, has partnered with venture capitalist and entrepreneur, Dr. Alex Mehr, to purchase distressed retail establishments. This digital marketing model is the model of the future as well as a way to generate income in the present.

<u>WHAT NEXT</u>

We have established that there is a formula for achieving a $1.2 million revenue in a year; it requires a direct-to-consumer approach. I recommend an online, as opposed to an offline, marketing strategy. So, what is the next step? You need a product. You need to advertise that product. You need to find an automated mechanism to get that product to the consumer. You also need to have a sales funnel, which can move consumers through a process at the end of which they will buy. Then, you need to have a mechanism in which people will buy monthly over time.

So, we are looking to create a base of five thousand consumers, who will spend $20 per month, over a 12-month period. Resulting in a $1.2 million revenue. We are taking a direct-to-consumer approach by means of online marketing. With online marketing, I am specifically referring to social media marketing, via Instagram, Facebook, Snapchat, or TikTok ads. For myself, I am going to focus on Facebook and Instagram ads. Whether we are talking online or offline marketing, there is a 1-3% response rate regarding direct-to-consumer advertising. So, we have to calculate the percentages that are required to reach 1%, 2% or 3% of the people to whom we are advertising, or better yet, achieving a 1%, 2% or 3% response rate. Additionally, it takes seven exposures to an ad for consumers to eventually buy. So again, it's all in the numbers. The formulas are precise because they are statistically driven.

The most important thing we need to do to achieve our goals and to accumulate one million dollars in one year is to have an idea for a product. As our formula says, we need to find five thousand consumers who will pay us $20 every month for a year. This may seem quite difficult, but I will explain to you how we can achieve it in practice. The most important thing is to get started. This is not about being perfect, for the important thing is the progress we make. You do not have to have a perfect product or a unique idea to build a working business, all you have to do is give value to people. For example, knowledge is the most valuable thing you can sell to people, and the truth is, they will give you a lot of money for it. You can start with an e-book, or take a short course on a topic you are familiar with. If you have knowledge that can be useful to people, no matter what it is, then you will be able to make money from it. Once you have an idea for a product, you need to find the people who need it. These are your ideal consumers. What is an ideal consumer you might ask? Well, before you can charge ahead and zone in on your target, you need to have a solid handle on what exactly an ideal consumer is. When you think about it this way, the entire concept is quite simple, your ideal consumer is someone who gets their exact needs met by what you are offering. To find your ideal consumers, you must first answer a few questions. Who would buy your product?

Who would find value in your product? How old is this person? What interests does this person have? What would your ideal consumer search on Google to find your product? Why does your ideal consumers need our product? Where does your ideal consumers look for a solution to the problems that your product can solve? Where do your ideal consumers look for information about products similar to yours? You need to get to know your consumers very well if you want to be successful in your sales. This will seem a bit complicated at first, but over time, some of the above questions will find an answer on their own. You need to be fully aware of exactly who you want to sell your products to in order to look for these people in the right places and meet the needs they have.

When you have a product that has value and you know who to sell it to, then all you have to do is present your product in the right way. This is the hard part. You need to convince people that your product is worth the money and will bring them a solution to their problem. If your product is well-crafted and can help people or teach them something, then selling it will not be an exceedingly challenging task. When you present your product, you are trying to convince your customers that this is their solution, and only this product is. Selling products to people who do not need them is not a sustainable strategy. This can even harm your business. The best way to convince someone that your product has value is to let them test it. To be able to feel it, smell it, touch it, and see it is part of the results; this way your customers will see for themselves the value of your product.

<u>SOME PRACTICAL WAYS</u>

Now, I will tell you about some practical ways to sell your products effectively. These methods have been tested over time, and if applied effectively and consistently, they will surely provide you with the required five thousand sales:

1. **Use your contacts**. Many people wonder where to start when they want to sell a product. Through social networks? Google marketing or YouTube marketing? Maybe email marketing? All these options are good, but we miss the most effective and most successful of them. Have you ever heard before the phrase, "The first customers of a start-up are always - friends,

family and fools?" This expression is not intended to offend your customers, but only to suggest that your first customers are your contacts. Tell your family and friends about what you do. Have them test or at least review your product and give you real feedback. In this way you can improve your product. You need to think of every possible person who could help you or recommend your product. Recommendations are an immensely powerful tool that you can use to your advantage. If you already have an audience on social networks, you should take advantage of that as well. For people to buy your products, they must first understand that they exist. If you make the first ten sales, many things will become clear to you about both the process and the product itself. To succeed, you need to talk about your product. You need to fully understand the Law of Attraction and take advantage of it.

2. **Use numbers**. Every sale is important to you, as well as to your potential customer. The more people buying your products, the more credible your product becomes. This is important because customers bring more customers with them. They recommend your

products, give positive feedback, and tell their friends, family, or followers about them. The best advertisement is a satisfied customer. If you tell people how many of your customers are happy with your products, or how many sales you have, it can help you sell your products. This is called the "sheep principle". Your potential customers are much more likely to trust people who have already used your products than you. Use numbers as a lever to increase your sales. Building a business is not an exact science, but it is mathematics. People trust the numbers behind your business because they can understand them. And if you have a thousand sales, then to your customers it means that someone has already tried your product and are most likely satisfied with it.

3. **The Four P's**. Now I will tell you about a successful and effective strategy with which you can make sales. This is part of the product presentation and is used when talking to your customers in person. This is a model by which you can conduct your sales and achieve remarkable success. It is especially important to meet the requirements and expectations

of customers when selling your products. It is important not only to make a sale, but also to fully understand your customers. Remember that you should only sell to people you believe need your products. Once you have made sure that these people have a real interest in your products, you need to move on to the sale. The Four P's model can help you in this process. This is a concept that will help you avoid getting lost in meaningless explanations about the qualities and advantages of your products.

- *Promise*. From the very beginning, you need to gain the full attention of your potential customers. They need to be extremely focused on what you tell them and not be distracted. The first fifteen seconds are the most important because you have just that much time to gain their attention. You need to make them want to hear more of what you have to say. They need to be interested in what you are saying. This way you will be sure that throughout the conversation your customers will be fully focused and will hear what you have to say. Start with a promise. Take

YouTube ads, for example. The people who create these ads spend the most time perfecting the first ten seconds of the ad. If they did not succeed, you will press the "skip ad" button. You will not even see the entire ad. On the other hand, if they managed to attract your attention in the first ten seconds, the chance to watch the whole ad and consider it increases many times over. These ads often catch people's attention with promises of something you will be able to do with that product or something you will know after using it. They show you the benefits of their product. This is your goal as well. You need to get your customers' attention with a promise. For example, "This product will cut your forest costs in half" or "After reading this e-book, you'll know how to make a million in a year!" You should make promises to people only if you are sure that they are possible. Do not lie to your customers!

- *Picture*. The next step is to draw the full picture in your clients' minds. Once you have attracted the attention of your customers, you need to move forward. Help them imagine how they will feel after using or reading your products. Paint the picture. For example, "A product like this can help you expand your knowledge in this area. It's useful to you because you can use it in your work and make money from that knowledge." Tell them a little about the benefits of your product that you think would be of most interest to your customers. Remember that it is extremely important that you first get to know and research your potential customers. This is the easiest way to meet their expectations. Most people often buy mostly on an emotional basis. That is more important for the customer. Make them feel the feelings they could feel if they used your products. It is more important for the customer to emotionally experience the product, than to know how useful it can actually be. This is about brand influence. Take, for example, major brands such as Nike and Adidas. What emotions do these brands evoke in you and why?

- **_Proof._** If you have done your job, your customers should already be emotionally attached to your product. They already know it well and have fully understood how this product can be useful and help them. But you also need proof of its effectiveness. You also need to prove in practice that your products are useful and have value. This can be done very easily and there are many ways to do it. With testimonials, or just letting customers use your products, as mentioned earlier. Here, you can use the numbers you have, as we said earlier in the book. Show them how satisfied your customers are and the benefits of using your products.

- **_Pitch_**. Once you have proven that your products are useful and your customers have an interest and benefit from them, you should proceed with closing the sale. If you have done your job well, this should not be a difficult stage for you. Just give guidance to your customers. If they are willing to buy from you, they will. Tell them what is next now that they are familiar with your products. You need to lead the meeting and guide the clients to the best choice for them.

4. **Customer behavior**. To be able to sell your products successfully and be successful in the long run, you need to understand your customers well. You need to understand their needs and wants, and always meet their expectations. You need to understand their buying behavior. What stages does each customer go through before deciding whether to buy exactly your product? What questions does he ask himself? Before making a purchase decision, each customer goes through the following phases:

- **Reaching**. To have a lot of sales, people need to know about your existence. Therefore, you need to reach them in some way - social networks, online marketing, email marketing. This is the customer's first contact with your product, and you should try to make it positive and captivating.

- **Collect information**. Once your potential customers have had their first encounter with your products, they need to know a little more about them before making a purchase. Here it is logical to think about where these people would look for information about our products- social networks, forums, blogs. Interacting with customers in such places can help you a lot in maintaining a good reputation. Give as much information as possible to your potential customers and acquaint them with your products, completely.

- **Comparison**. Often before making a purchase decision, our potential customers compare the alternatives. Look for others similar to your products, compare prices and quality. As I said, you do not have to have a perfect or new product to sell it successfully, but you do have to try to be better at something than the competition. This could be a bonus to the products, a warranty, additional content variety, or so on. Your competition is also your innovative engine. In the business world, you always have to have a competitive advantage to be successful in the long run. Give more than customers expect.

- **Purchase decision**. Once they have gathered all the available information and reviewed it quickly, your customers must make a final decision. You need to provide them with all the possible ways and means by which your customers can get your product. Give them a choice and guide them on who is right for them. You must facilitate the process of purchasing the product as much as possible. Did you know that 84% of online sales that have not been fully realized are due to problems at the checkout page?

THE FINAL WORDS

5,000 x 20 x 12 Strategy = Create Products/Services which pay $20/month for 12 months.

Here is the beauty of this formula: You can multiply it by ten to scale from one $1 million in revenue, to $1billion in revenue. I am sharing this with you, because I believe that this e-book is the only one that you will ever need to read. Check this out:

- 5,000 x 20 x 12 or 5,000 x 240 = $1,200,000
- 50,000 x 20 x 12 or 50,000 x 240 = $12,000,000
- 500,000 x 20 x 12 or 500,000 x 240 = $120,000,000

- 5,000,000 x 20 x 12 or 5,000,000 x 240 = $1,200,000,000

I have shown you The Formula, as well as the strategies. I have also shown you the formulas to increase your revenue by the power of 10. I want to extend my gratitude, as well as give a shout-out, to my social media consultant, Kristiyan Popov. If you need a Superlative Consultant for your social media marketing and strategy, hit him up via *Upwork.com*.

Your success as an Internet Entrepreneur will be driven by several factors, one of which is your willingness to make a financial commitment to fund your venture. As it is said, "You have to have 'skin in the game.'" That "skin" is your money. Yes, it is possible to use OPM (Other Peoples' Money). Yet, any Investor - Angel Investor / Venture Capitalist/Bank/Other, will want to know that you have made a financial commitment to your own success. To help you to understand the financial commitment needed to invest in your venture(s), we will be creating tools and resources for you. **Stay tuned!**

www.ingramcontent.com/pod-product-compliance
Lightning Source LLC
Chambersburg PA
CBHW071526180526
45171CB00002B/395